nF419407

TO:

FROM:

MOM

I LOVE YOU TO THE BEACH AND MORE

Becki A. Jacobson

BECKI ORIGINALS PUBLISHING

MOM
I Love You to the Beach and More

Published by Becki Originals Publishing
23 East Main Street #0426
Mystic, Connecticut 06355

Printed in the United States of America

Paperback ISBN: 979-8-9903319-4-5
Hardcover ISBN: 979-8-9903319-1-4

DEDICATION

TO MY MOM,
WHO MIRACULOUSLY FINDS A WAY
TO MAKE THE BEACH FEEL SUNNY
ON A RAINY DAY.

and more ...

Mom,
I love you to the beach and more.
I know I told you
I loved you before.

But I want to make sure you know
just how deep my feelings go.

They go deep into the sea
and settle in the sand.

They include my first memories
of holding your hand.

Sharing laughs with you
as the days go by.

Leaning in on your shoulders
when I cry.

You are my constant
when I hit a wave.

You are my cheerleader
when it's hard to feel brave.

You help me overcome
and conquer the sea.
Whenever I am lost,
you bring me back to me.

You are the sail that lifts my smile.
Your loving way radiates style.

And somehow,
you miraculously find a way
to make the beach feel sunny
on a rainy day.

I Love You

Mom,
I know I told you I loved you before.
But now you know
I love you to the beach and more!

Mom, I love you!

I appreciate you taking the time to read my book!

I hope you keep following my stories and my real-life adventures with my rescue dog, Murphy! If you liked this book, kindly share your feedback on Amazon.com at https://www.amazon.com/author/becki-jacobson.

To arrange a visit or event, please contact me directly at becki@beckijacobson.com and explore my website at beckijacobson.com. Stay tuned for more books like this and Murphy and Me adventure books in progress – I look forward to sharing our latest updates with you!

Other books by Becki:

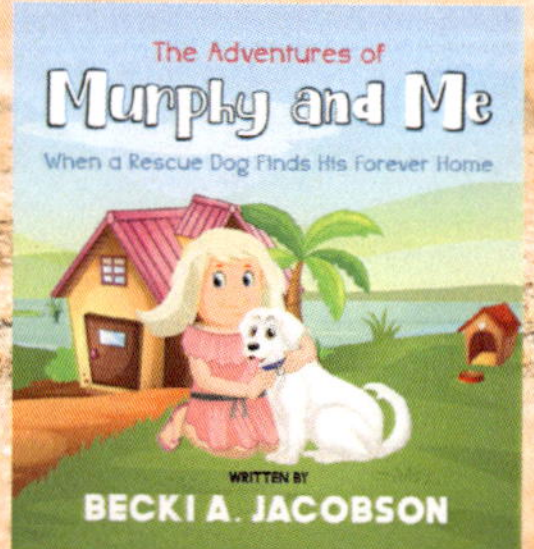

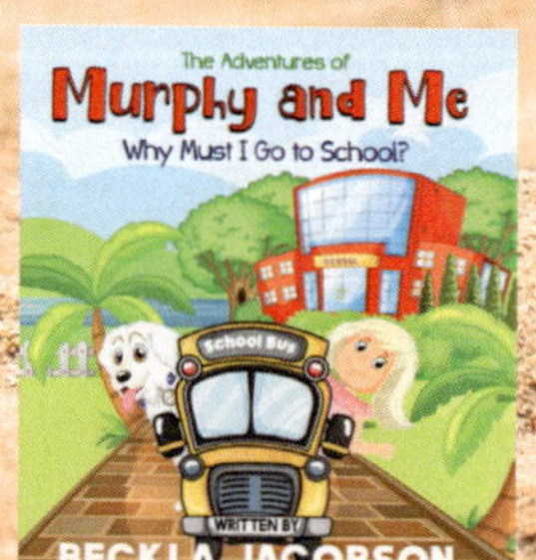

About the Author

Becki A. Jacobson, a true Connecticut native, shaped her roots in Canterbury before diving into the legal world. Now, she's a legal maverick serving clients near and far, based on the picturesque Mystic coast. When she's not conquering legal battles, she's busy crafting stories and exploring with her loyal sidekick, Murphy.

To uncover more about her world, check out her website at beckijacobson.com or drop her a line at becki@beckijacobson.com.

Looking forward to hearing from you soon!

~ Becki